Doris Kutschbach

# The Great ART Treasure Hunt

## Treasure Hunt

## I Spy Red, Yellow, and Blue

**PRESTEL**   Munich · London · New York

# What is
## your favorite color?

**Let´s take a journey of discovery into the world of pictures.**
This big art book is filled with different colors for you to explore.

**Would you like to come along?**

I spy with my little eye ...
**something ...**

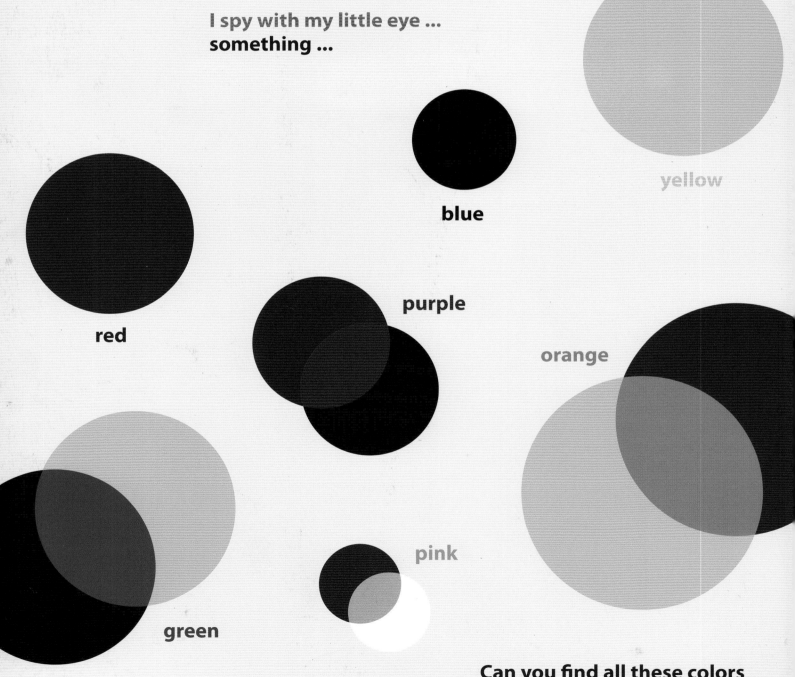

yellow

**blue**

**purple**

**red**

orange

pink

**green**

**Can you find all these colors in the picture on the right?**

# Fighting colors

**Red and blue look almost like wild animals.**

- **Isn't that a dark bird's beak?**
- **Could those be red claws?**

In this picture red and blue are very large and wild. But can you also find other colors?

# Yellow is warm

The summer sun saturates this picture in yellow. Can you feel its warmth?

Can you find a scythe, women bundling grain, a hay cart, one man drinking from a jug and another climbing a tree, a sailboat, a church, a basket with bread, two birds?

# Green, green, green ...

**The meadow looks fresh and lush.**
**Children are playing between the trees.**

Do you see the girl picking flowers? The women laying white washing out in the grass to dry? Can you find a man with a wheelbarrow?

# Ice cold in snowy white

I spy with my little eye …

a horse-drawn sled on the ice, a white dog, ice hockey players, a roof on fire. People are fetching water to put it out, a man is breaking a hole in the ice. A woman has fallen down.

What else can you discover?

# A golden hoard

Adele's dress is decorated with real gold and silver and lots of different patterns.

Can you find these details in the big picture?

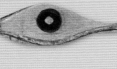

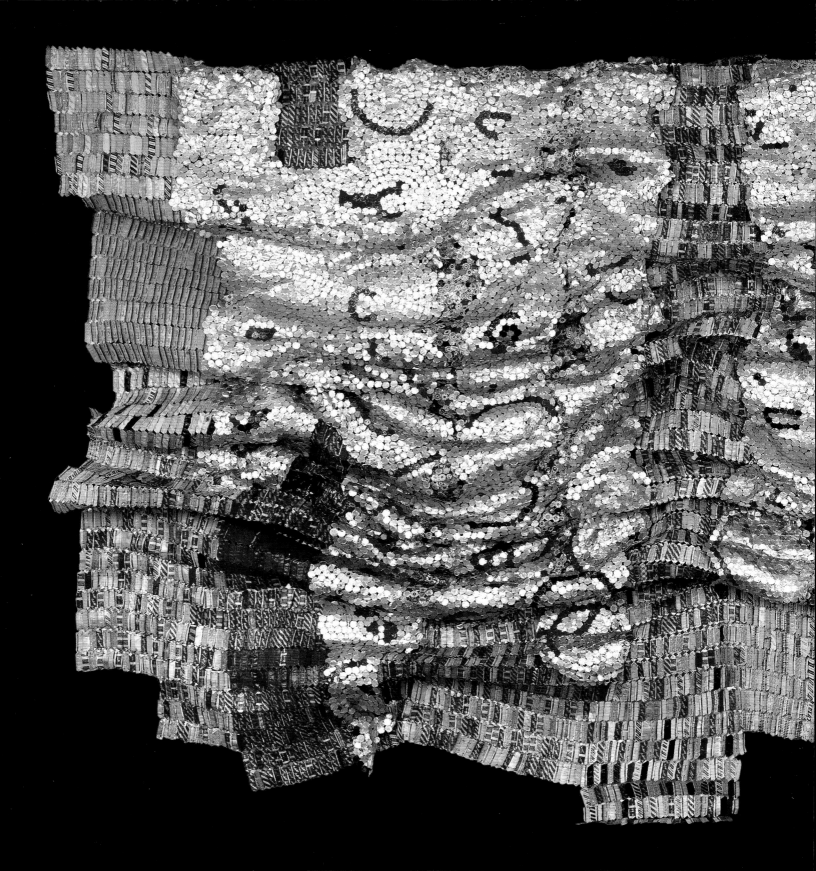

A carpet of colored tin

**The artist made it with old tin cans.**
See if you can find these places ...

# Brightly colored

## I spy with my little eye ...

- **a red biplane**
- **a brown bird**
- **a green bridge**
- **a red propeller**
- a yellow wheel
- **a red tower**

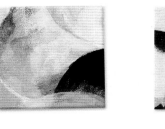

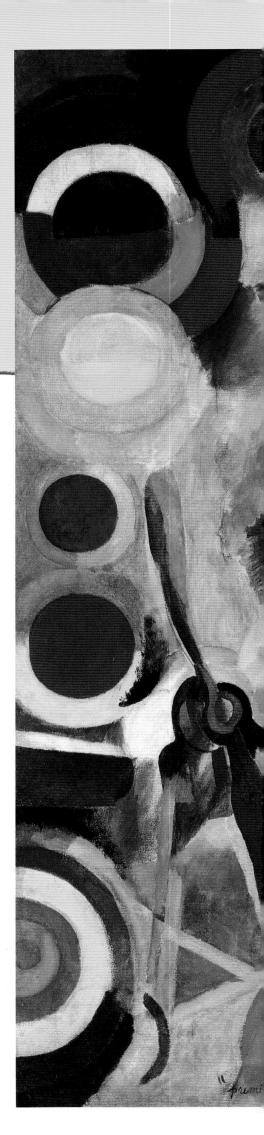

**The artist Hundertwasser
loved the way colors look on a rainy day.**

HUNDERTWASSER

**Can you find**

- **the man with the striped hat,**

- **the little house with a green roof,**

- **the checkered car,**

- **a red and yellow onion dome,**

- **the bicyclist?**

**What else can you find?**

# Colors
## like earth, sand, and clay

Hey, who ran through this picture? Can you find
the tracks made by the emu and the snake?

Can you think of any other animals that live in Australia?

- emu
- snake
- gecko
- dingo
- koala bear
- spiny anteater
- kangaroo

# A colorful underwater world

The algae have been cut out of colored paper.
- Can you find the red algae on a green background?
- And the yellow algae on a blue background?

Which fish go with which algae?
And which combinations are not in the picture above?

# Broad brushstrokes

The painter Vincent van Gogh painted his bedroom with a broad brush in thick, intense colors.

Can you find these places in the big picture?

# Point by point

This whole picture has been made out of tiny dots of paint.

Can you find these details in the big picture?

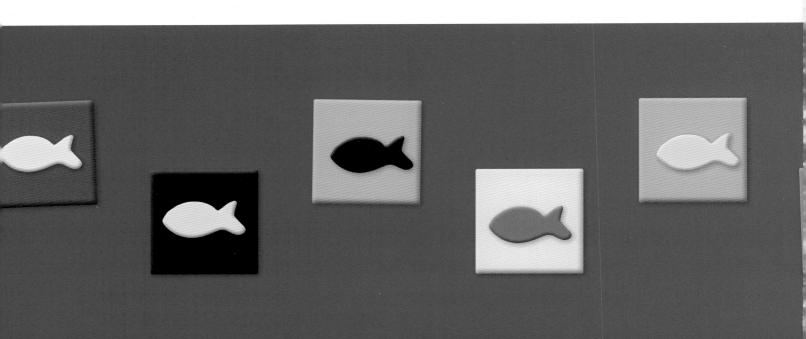

# On the water

This summertime picture of catching crayfish on the shore was painted with watercolors.

I spy
with my little eye …
… something …

• as blue as water

• as green as grass

• **as red as a crayfish**

# A drip painting

**Here a few paint cans seem to have sprung leaks!**
**Can you find these colors in the big picture?**

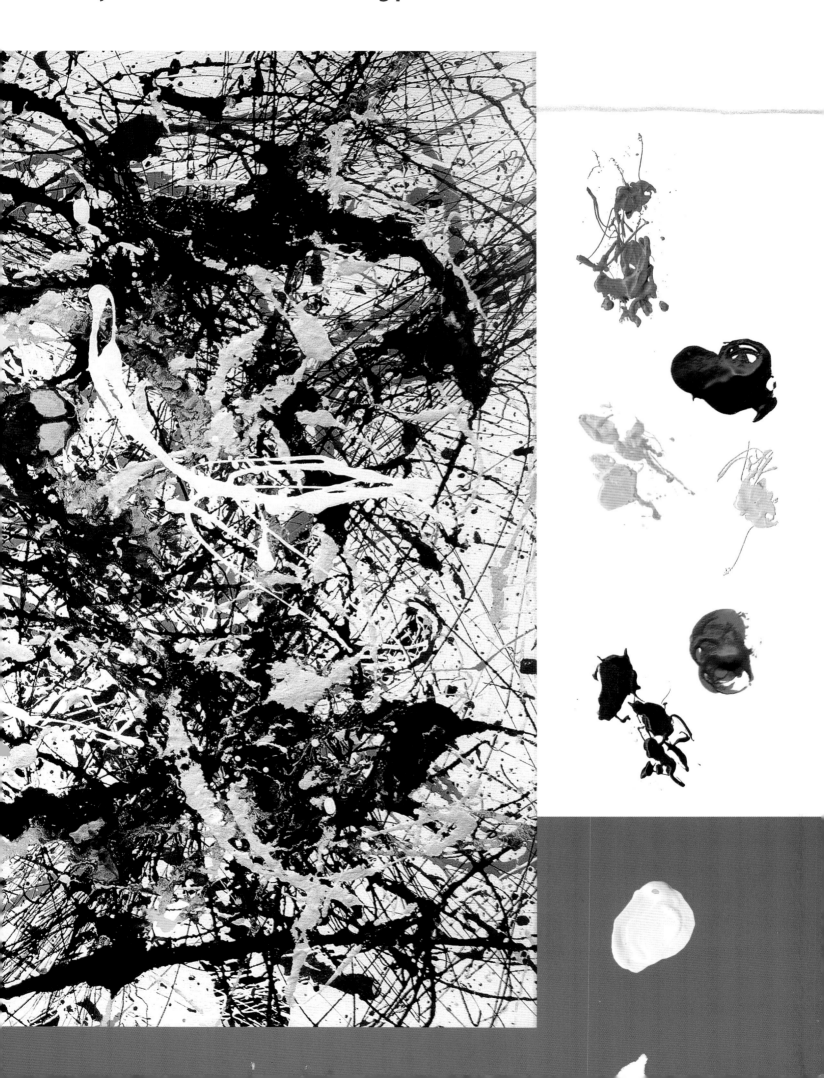

# In the Garden of Eden

Paradise seems to be inhabited by some strange animals. They've all been painted carefully with fine brushes. You can make everything out very clearly.

Can you find

- the giraffe with its long neck,

- the bear climbing a tree,

- a snake, an owl, and a unicorn,

- the wild boar's babies,

- a two-legged dog,

- a lion eating lunch,

- a three-headed lizard,

- and a porcupine?


**What animal is the monkey riding?**

**Can you find these animals in the big picture?**

# A carpet of colorful threads

**A pattern of animals and plants has been woven into this tapestry:**

**Can you find**

- **a monkey,**

- **a magpie,**

- **a lamb,**

- **a unicorn?**

- **How many little rabbits can you find?**

**Where are these plants and fruits?**

oranges

violets

red berries

white daisies

yellow daffodils

forget-me-nots

red carnations

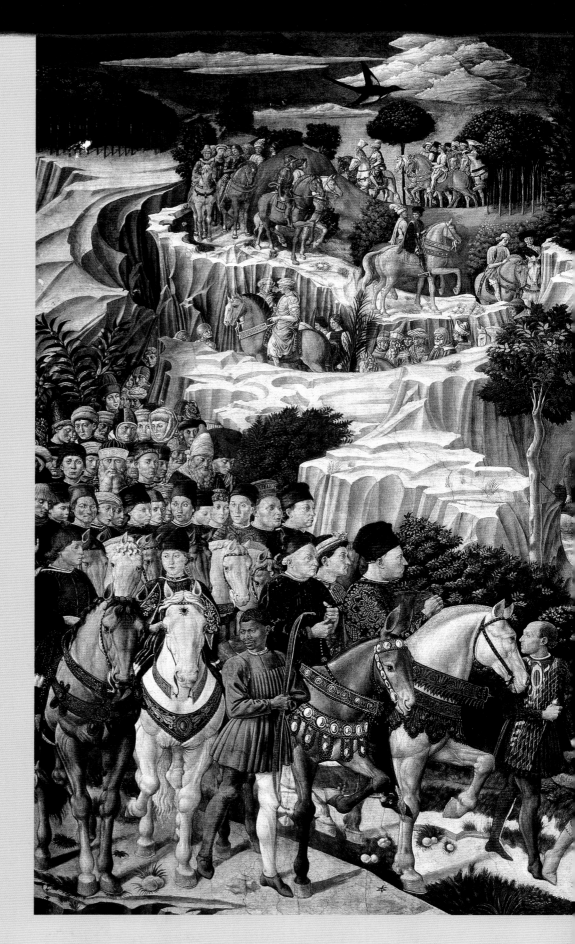

# Is it real or is it painted?

Many exotic birds can be seen in the display case.
Maybe you know one by name?

The big blue parrot stands out right away. But can you also find

- an orange bird,

- a little green egg,

- the bird with the dark plumage and blue cheeks,

- and the bird with the yellow belly with red stripes?

- One with a yellow belly,

- and one with a striped beak?

Can you also find

- the little red-brown bird with the bright red beak,

- the largest egg,

- the smallest egg?

Whose shadows are these?

# Hustle and bustle
# on the canal

**Can you find**

**a white cat, a red gondola with men in fisherman's trousers, a puppy, an oarsman in blue pants, a girl with a red skirt?**

**What else do you see?**

# In the darkness all cats are gray

- The trees and fields are gray-green.

- The roofs are grayish-brown.

- The river is gray-blue.

- **Only the windows glow bright yellow.**

- **A messenger is galloping through the dark night – can you see him?**

- **Lights have gone on in the houses.**

- **People are coming out of their houses. They are wearing white nightshirts.**

- A child is running to the neighbors' house.

- Someone is looking out the window.

- **Can you see another village in the distance?**

# The pictures in this book

**1** August Macke
**Turkish Café II** (1914)

Oil on wood, 60 × 35 cm · Munich, Lenbachhaus
Photo: Artothek

August Macke (1887–1914) is one of the most famous Expressionist artists. He lived in Cologne and belonged to the inner circle of artists around Franz Marc. Sadly, he died at a young age during the First World War. In his picture of the café, he makes the colors glow intensely by combining them with their complements: red is next to green, blue next to orange, and yellow next to purple.

**2** Franz Marc
**Fighting Forms** (1914)

Oil on canvas, 91 x 131.5 cm · Munich, Pinakothek der Moderne
Photo: Blauel/Gnamm – Artothek

Franz Marc (1880–1916) was a close friend of Macke's and co-founder of the artists' group The Blue Rider. He painted almost only pictures of animals. In this picture the colors red and blue play the leading roles. A wild fight is taking place without any recognizable objects.

But with a lot of imagination the forms can also be interpreted as a bird's beak and red claws, a red nose, a sheep's head, or a thick tail.

**3** Pieter Bruegel the Elder
**The Harvesters** (1565)

Oil on wood, 118 x 161 cm · New York, Metropolitan Museum of Art
Photo: akg-images

The Netherlandish painter Pieter Bruegel the Elder (c. 1525–1569) is famous for his highly-detailed pictures that show us the everyday life of people in the Middle Ages. *The Harvesters* is one of his series of the Seasons and represents high summer. The saturated yellow of the ripe grain makes it possible for you to literally feel the warm summer day.

**4** Max Liebermann
**Children Playing in the Park** (1882)

Oil on canvas, 51 x 69 cm · private collection
Photo: Christie's Images Ltd – Artothek

Green plays the leading role in this bright picture of children happily playing in the park. The Berlin artist Max Liebermann (1847–1935) was a famous Impressionist painter. The lightheartedness of this picture makes it hard to imagine the shadows that would later cross the artist's life. As a Jew, Liebermann could not work under the Nazis and towards the end of his life he retreated completely from public life.

**5** Lucas van Valckenborch
**Winter Landscape with Snowfall near Antwerp** (1575)

Oil on oak, 61 x 82.5 cm · Frankfurt am Main, Städel Museum
Photo: U. Edelmann · Städel Museum – Artothek

White, gray, and light blue are the cold colors of winter and in this picture you can see exactly what people in the Middle Ages did at this time of year. Lucas van Valckenborch (c. 1535–1597) was a Flemish painter. Like his older colleague, Pieter Breugel, he painted the seasons, festivals, rural activities and work, and the everyday life of the people.

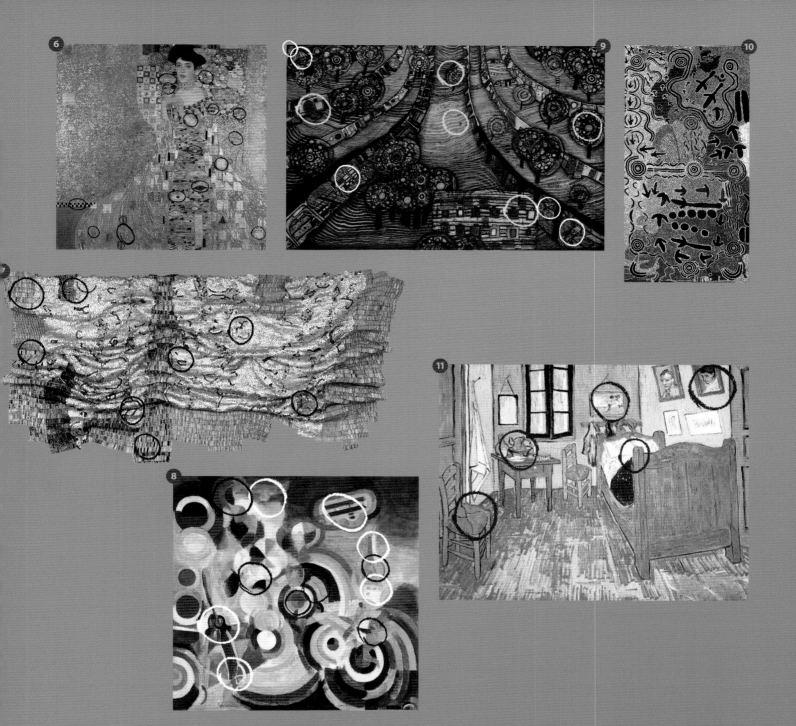

**6 Gustav Klimt**
**Portrait of Adele Bloch-Bauer I** (1907)

Oil, gold, and silver on canvas, 138 x 138 cm · New York,
Neue Galerie. Photo: Artothek

Jugendstil, or Art Nouveau, loved luxurious
ornament, especially in Vienna, where Gustav
Klimt (1862–1918) was the most sought-after
artist of the affluent society and ladies stood
in line to be painted by him. In this portrait,
he painted the rich industrialist's wife Adele
Bloch-Bauer with real gold and silver. The whole
picture is covered with a glittering pattern; only
the sitter's hand and eyes seem to be of flesh
and blood.

**7 El Anatsui**
**Awu** (2009)

Aluminium and copper wire,  503 x 762 cm · New York,
Jack Shainman Gallery. Photo: Jack Shainman Gallery

El Anatsui was born in Ghana in 1944 and has
lived in Nigeria longer than anywhere else. His
installation covers the whole wall like a precious
textile. If you look carefully, you can see why it's
so sparkly: old cans, pieces of sheet metal, and
packaging material are joined together with
wires into a magnificent tin carpet.

**8 Robert Delaunay**
**Hommage à Blériot** (1914)

Glue tempera on canvas, 250.5 x 251.5 cm · Basel, Kunstmuseum
Photo: Hans Hinz – Artothek

Robert Delaunay (1885–1941) was the most
important representative of the art movement
known as Orphism. The world of this picture is
composed of brightly colored circles, between
which can be seen the Eiffel Tower, airplanes,
and other objects. Delaunay's pictures are
characterized by intense colors—a sensation
at the time, for back then art was dominated
by much more muted colors.

**9 Friedensreich Hundertwasser**
**781 Green Town**

Mixed media, Venice, 1978, 97 x 145 cm · private collection

Friedensreich Hundertwasser (1928–2000) also
gave himself the names Regentag (Rainy Day)
and Dunkelbunt (Darkly Multi-colored), since on
a rainy day the colors seem to glow especially
brightly against the darkness. He painted in
pure, deeply glowing colors, his pictures taking
form like slowly grow-ing plants in nature.
Protecting the environment was very important
to him and he thought that people should live
in harmony with nature.

**10 Darby Jampijinpa Ross**
**Yankiri Jukurrpa** (Emu dreaming) (1986)

Acrylic paint on cotton  · Art Gallery of New South Wales,
Sydney, Australia / Gift of the Art Gallery Society of New South
Wales 1995. Photo: The Bridgeman Art Library

Darby Jampijinpa Ross (1910–2005) painted his
picture in warm, earthy colors. The Australians
have a close connection to their land. Pictures
like these used to be painted with earth pig-
ments but today the artists often use acrylic
paints. The circles could represent watering
holes, or trees or hills; in between snake tracks
can be seen. The emu is a very common bird in
Australia. Its tracks in this picture are typical of
this large bird, which cannot fly.

**11 Vincent van Gogh**
**Van Gogh's Bedroom in Arles** (1888)

Oil on canvas, 72 x 90 cm · Paris, Musée d'Orsay
Photo: Peter Willi – Artothek

Vincent van Gogh (1853–1898) painted his most
beautiful and colorful pictures in the sunny light
of southern France. His *Bedroom in Arles* glows in
sparkling colors. You can clearly see how thickly
he applied the oil paint to the canvas—this is
called impasto. It's completely different from the
delicate, transparent watercolors of Carl Larsson's
painting.

**These fish do not match any algae.**

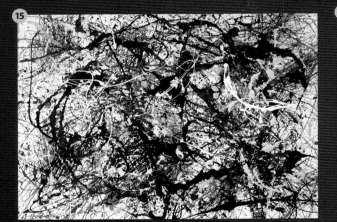

**The monkey is riding an elephant.**

**12** Henri Matisse
**Composition** (1947)

Gouache, cut-out, 52 x 218 cm · Basel, Kunstmuseum
Photo: Hans Hinz - Artothek

Henri Matisse lived from 1869 to 1954 and was one of the most important artists of the twentieth century. This picture, which is almost two-and-a-half meters long, is a cut-out: To make it, the artist first colored sheets of paper with paint and then cut the forms directly out of the paper with scissors. He called it "drawing with scissors."

**13** Paul Signac
**The Port of St. Tropez** (1923)

Oil on canvas, 60 x 73 cm · private collection
Photo: Christie's Images Ltd – Artothek

This kind of painting is called "pointillism": Paul Signac (1863–1935) composed his pictures of very many small dots of color. The trick is that the colors become mixed in the eye of the viewer. Seen from up close, for example, an orange-colored area turns out to be made up of yellow and red dots that are painted very close to one another.

**14** Carl Larsson
**The Crayfish Season Opens** (1897)

Watercolor, 32 x 43 cm · Stockholm, Nationalmuseum
Photo: akg-images

In the late summer Sweden celebrate the crayfish festival. The Swedish artist Carl Larsson (1853–1919) has used delicate, transparent colors to paint his family catching crawfish. In the foreground is his daughter Lisbeth, and behind her are the artist's wife Karin and the youngest, Kersti. On the lake are Ulf, Pontus, and Brita, and Suzanne in the boat.

**15** Jackson Pollock
**Number 34** (1949)

Oil and enamel on white cardboard, mounted on board, 56 x 78 cm · New York, Munson-Williams-Proctor Inst.
Photo: akg-images / Cameraphoto

What Jackson Pollock (1912–1956) did with paints was truly exciting: He filled the liquid paint in cans with holes in the bottom and let it drip onto the surface of the canvas. These "drip paintings" are meant to be determined by chance, not by the artist's hand guiding a brush. And this is how "Jack the Dripper" (his nickname) became the founder of Action Painting.

**16** Hieronymus Bosch
**Paradise** (detail) (c. 1500)

Oil on wood, triptych, 220 x 195 cm · Madrid,
Museo del Prado. Photo: Artothek

The Netherlandish artist Hieronymus Bosch (c. 1450–1516) was a master of fine oil painting. His pictures are filled with puzzles and today no one knows anymore just how to interpret them. *Paradise,* of which only the upper half is shown here, is part of a three-part altarpiece. Hieronymus Bosch filled his paradise with strange fantastic beings painted with a fine brush in delicate colors.

**17** **The Lady with the Unicorn: Allegory of Smell**
(between 1484 and 1500)

Tapistry, 312 x 330 cm · Paris, Musée Cluny
Photo: Peter Willi – Artothek

This is one of six precious tapestries with representations of the senses; this one is smell. For valuable tapestries such as these, threads of wool and silk—and sometimes even gold and silver—were woven together to make pictures. The pattern of tiny strewn flowers is called "millefleurs."

**18** Benozzo Gozzoli
**Detail from the Three Wise Men** (1459–61)

Wall painting · Florence, Palazzo Medici Riccardi
Photo: Alinari – Artothek

Benozzo Gozzoli (c. 1420–1497) painted three whole walls of the Medici family chapel with the procession of the Three Wise Men. Wall paintings such as these are called frescos after the Italian word "fresco" (= fresh), because the paint is applied directly into the fresh, wet plaster, making these paintings very durable. That's also why the colors in this artwork still look so fresh despite how old it is.

**19** Alexandre-Isidore Leroy de Barde
**Collection of Exotic Birds** (1810)

Watercolor and gouache, 126 x 90 cm · Paris,
Musée du Louvre. Photo: RMN / Jean-Gilles Berizzi

The birds in this display case, painted by Alexandre-Isidore Leroy de Barde (1777–1825), look deceptively real, almost as if the painting were a photograph of stuffed birds. At the time, almost 200 years ago, many explorers travelled to distant lands in order to research the strange animal and plant worlds. Collectors scrambled to acquire the animals, plants, shells, and other exotic things that the explorers brought back. And since photography and film had not yet been invented, painters like this one depicted the discoveries very painstakingly.

**20** Canaletto (Giovanni Antonio Canal)
**Regatta on the Grand Canal, View from Ca' Foscari** (c. 1740)

Oil on canvas, 115.5 x 174 cm · London, National Gallery
Photo: Peter Willi · Artothek

When the first tourists streamed into Venice in the eighteenth century, this was just fine with Giovanni Antonio Canal, called Canaletto (1697–1768). He was the best painter of vedutte (city views) of his time and the tourists enthusiastically snapped up his pictures as souvenirs, since photographs did not yet exist. Even today the exact representation of each detail is still astonishing.

**21** Grant Wood
**The Midnight Ride of Paul Revere** (1931)

Oil on board, 76.2 x 101.6 cm · New York,
The Metropolitan Museum of Art
Photo: bpk | The Metropolitan Museum of Art

Paul Revere is a hero of the American Revolution. In his dramatic recreation, Grant Wood (1891–1942) tells the story of Paul Revere´s midnight ride from Boston to Cambridge to warn the American people of the approaching British troops. The only bright color here is the yellow light; all the other colors become gray in the darkness of night.

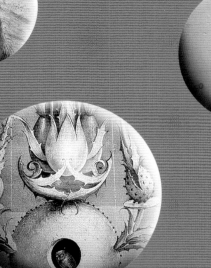

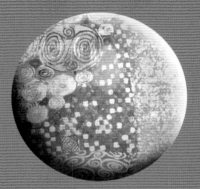

© **Prestel Verlag, Munich – London – New York, 2013**
© for the reproduced works by Darby Jampijinpa Ross and
Grant Wood: VG Bild-Kunst, Bonn 2013; Jackson Pollock: Pollock-
Krasner Foundation/VG Bild-Kunst, Bonn 2013; Henri Matisse:
Succession H. Matisse/VG Bild-Kunst, Bonn 2013; Friedensreich
Hundertwasser: 2013 NAMIDA AG, Glarus/Schweiz; El Anatsui:
Jack Shainman Gallery 2013.

Prestel, a member of Verlagsgruppe Random House GmbH

Prestel Verlag, Munich
www.prestel.de

Prestel Publishing Ltd.
14-17 Wells Street
London W1T 3PD

Prestel Publishing
900 Broadway, Suite 603
New York, NY 10003

**www.prestel.com**

Library of Congress Control Number is available; British Library
Cataloguing-in-Publication Data: a catalogue record for this book is
available from the British Library; Deutsche Nationalbibliothek holds
a record of this publication in the Deutsche Nationalbibliografie;
detailed bibliographical data can be found under: http://dnb.ddb.de

Prestel books are available worldwide. Please contact your nearest
bookseller or one of the above addresses for information concerning
your local distributor.

Front cover: detail from Hieronymus Bosch, *Paradise*
Back cover: detail from Robert Delaunay, *Hommage à Blériot*

Picture selection and text: Doris Kutschbach
Translation and copy-editing: Cynthia Hall
Design: Katarzyna Roy
Design concept and cover: SOFAROBOTNIK, Augsburg & Munich
Production: Astrid Wedemeyer
Art direction: Cilly Klotz
Lithography: Reproline Mediateam, Munich
Printing and binding: Tien Wah, Malaysia

FSC
www.fsc.org
MIX
Paper from
responsible sources
FSC® C012700

Verlagsgruppe Random House FSC® N001967
The FSC®-certified paper *HannoArt Silk* is produced
by mill Sappi, Alfeld.

ISBN 978-3-7913-7106-1